TEN POTATOES IN A POT
——And Other Counting Rhymes——

Selected by Michael Jay Katz
Pictures by June Otani

HARPER & ROW, PUBLISHERS

Library of Congress Cataloging-in-Publication Data
Ten potatoes in a pot and other counting rhymes / selected by Michael
Jay Katz : pictures by June Otani.
         p.   cm.
   Summary: A collection of traditional counting rhymes, including
both popular and little-known verses.
     ISBN 0-06-023106-8 : $. — ISBN 0-06-023107-6 (lib. bdg.) :
$
     1. Nursery rhymes. 2. Children's poetry. [1. Nursery rhymes.
2. Counting.] I. Katz, Michael Jay, 1950-   . II. Otani, June ,
ill.
PZ8.3.K1285Te 1990   89-15583
[E]—dc20   CIP
                                                              AC

To my children, Emily and Ethan
—M.J.K.

To Miyoko, Hiroshi, and Robert
—J.O.

1	2	3	4	5	6	7	8	9	10
11	12	13	14	15	16	17	18	19	20

One, two—buckle my shoe.
Three, four—shut the door.
Five, six—pick up sticks;
Seven, eight—lay them straight.
Nine, ten—a good, fat hen.
Eleven, twelve—dig and delve.
Thirteen, fourteen—maids a-courting;
Fifteen, sixteen—maids a-kissing;
Seventeen, eighteen—maids a-waiting;
Nineteen, twenty—maids a-plenty.

One-year-old little son,
Now his life has just begun.
Do you think he'll have some fun?
Not until he learns to run.

One bun is overdone—
Coat it quick with cinnamon,
Set it in the morning sun,
Then eat it when the day is done.

Two little birds sitting on a stone:
One flew away—he went home;
The other flew next—to parts unknown;
And now the stone is all alone.

Muffins, muffins, two for a penny—
Tommy got sick from eating too many.
One and one buys a two-penny bread,
Or two little one-penny hotbuns instead.

Baa, baa, black sheep,
Have you any wool?
Yes, sir, yes, sir,
Three bags full:
One for the master,
One for the dame,
And one for the little boy
Who lives down the lane.

Hinty, minty, cutty, corn,
Apple seed and apple thorn;
Fire, briar, limber-lock,
Three old geese flew in a flock—
One flew east, and one flew west,
And one flew over the cuckoo's nest.

They flew up onto yonder hill
Where my father has his mill.
He has a hammer with three nails;
He has a cat that has three tails;
He has three jewels; he has three rings;
He has three other pretty things.

One, two, three, four—
Mary's at the kitchen door,
Picking cherries off the floor,
Hoping they won't fall once more.

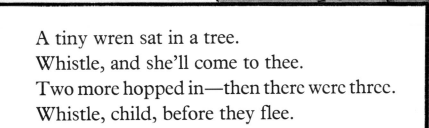

A tiny wren sat in a tree.
Whistle, and she'll come to thee.
Two more hopped in—then there were three.
Whistle, child, before they flee.

Another came, and there were four
But you needn't whistle anymore;
For, being frightened, off they flew,
And none are left to play with you.

One, two, three, and four, and five,
I saw a fishie take a dive;
I caught the fishie, still alive.

"What made you let the fishie go?"
Because it bit my finger so.
"And which finger did it bite?"
My little finger on the right.

One and one are two;
Two and one are three.
We started for the fair,
Jennifer, John, and me.

Three and one are four;
Four and one are five.
Our horse has lost his way—
Will we ever arrive?

One cup, two cups, sometimes three—
You love coffee; I love tea.
Four cups, five cups, even six—
Drink them alone, 'cause they don't mix.

Wink, mink, a pepper drink,
A baby bottle full of ink.
One and one and one are three:
Let's choose sides; out goes he.

Apples, oranges, yellow pears,
Sitting on the kitchen chairs.
Two and two and two are six:
He chooses you; you're the one he picks.

As I was going to St. Ives,
I met a man with seven wives.
Each wife had seven sacks;
Each sack had seven cats;
Each cat had seven kits.
Kits, cats, sacks, and wives—
How many were going to St. Ives?

Only me!

One, two, three, four, five, six, seven—
All good children go to Heaven.
Some go up and some go down,
And some go all around the town.
A penny by horsecart, two pennies by sea,
Three pennies by railway, but Heaven is free.

One, two, three, four—
Preacher's at the chapel door.
Five, six, seven, eight—
Wondering who will come in late.
In comes Cat, in comes Rat,
In comes Lady with the great big hat.

Monkey, monkey, barrel of beer—
How many monkeys are in here?
One or two or three or four—
Put a monkey out the door.
Five or six or seven or eight—
Too many monkeys; I'll just wait.

One and two and three and four—
Mommy scrubbed the kitchen floor.
Five, six, seven, eight, and nine—
The kitchen dried, so we could dine.

9

If you listen, I'll sing you a song,
And I would guess that it's nine verses long—
I'll give you a pin if I've guessed wrong.

Three and three and three are nine—
And if I don't forget a line,
I guess the pin will still be mine.

Mingle-dee, pingle-dee, clap-clap-clap—
How many fingers do I hold in my lap?
  Would you say one?
  Would you say two?
    Raspberries, strawberries,
    Fresh with the dew.
  Would you say three?
  Would you say four?
    Rutabaga, pumpkins,
    Onions and corn.
  Would you say five?
  Would you say six?
    Dandelions, crocuses,
    Chicory sticks.
  Would you say seven?
  Would you say eight?
    Eggs and cheese muffins
    On a dinner plate.
  Would you say nine?
  Would you say ten?
    Then open your eyes
    And count them all again.
Mingle-dee, pingle-dee, clap-clap-clap—
How many fingers do I hold in my lap?

Ten potatoes in a pot,
Take two out and eight stay hot.
Eight potatoes in the pan,
Take two out, there's six to plan.
Six potatoes on the stove,
Take two off and four's the trove.
Four potatoes in the kettle,
Take two out, leave two to settle.
Two potatoes still aboil,
Take them out before they spoil.

Eleven comets in the sky,
Some flew low and some flew high.
Nine grey geese were in the air;
I wonder how they all came there.
Seven lobsters in a dish,
As fresh as any heart could wish.
Five black beetles on the wall
By an apple woman's stall.
Three brown horses in a bog;
Their cart is stuck beside a frog—
One gaping, wide-mouthed, waddling frog,
Watching comets from a log.

One, I love,
Two, you love,
Three, I love—I say.
Four, we love with all our hearts,
Let's never go away.

Five, I court,
Six, you court,
Seven, I court—I say.
Eight, we court from the very start,
Holding hands and gay.

Nine, I marry,
Ten, you marry,
Eleven, I marry—I say.
Twelve, we marry and never part
From our wedding day.

High on a hillside
Brown as bread,
Emmy found a berry patch
Spotted all in red.

Raspberries, raspberries,
Thick as fireflies,
Dotting all the bushes
Like stars in the skies.

"One, two, twenty, sixty deep—
A fifteen hundred berry heap."
Emmy tried to count them all
But soon she fell asleep.